CIRCLE OF HELMETS

Poetry and Letters of the Vietnam War

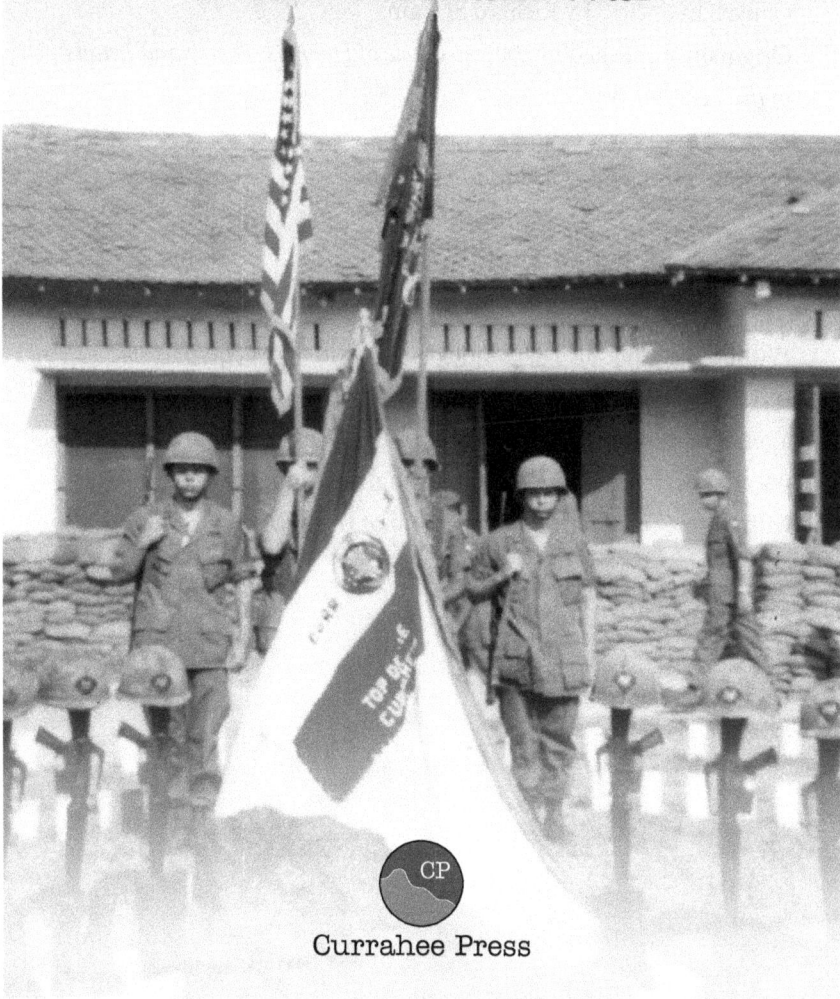

CP

Currahee Press

Currahee Press LLC
1639 Bradley Park Drive
Suite 500/366, Columbus, Georgia 31904

Second Edition Paperback 2017
Copyright © 2017 by Richard St John
Originally published in 2002 as *Circle of Helmets: Poetry and Letters of the Vietnam War.*

ISBN: 978-0-9988542-4-3

Copyright in process

Cover photo: Rick St John

Design: Toelke Asssociates
www.toelkeassociates.com

This book is dedicated in loving memory to my parents, Brigadier General William J. St John (US Army, retired) and Mary G. St John.

CONTENTS

PREFACE

For thirty years I avoided my memories of the Vietnam War. It wasn't so much that the memories were painful; it was more that I didn't want to discover if they would be. Hence, my avoidance of anything having to do with what was a life altering experience for a young, impressionable soldier. Then something happened — memories started to bubble up on their own! My defense mechanisms so carefully honed over the decades no longer worked. I couldn't suppress the thoughts anymore. To my surprise the memories were painful yes, but in a cathartic way. I began to nurture and cultivate this newfound experience. At about this same time I discovered poetry — what a perfect fit! On the one hand a rich source of emotions and pain, and on the other the poetic medium which feeds off just such deep emotions.

One of my first poems was Journey Home. Early on I realized that keeping my Vietnam memories and experiences in check kept me from being a full, complete and open person. In a matter of months, I had amassed notebooks full of ideas, catchy phrases and poems. Then, I rediscovered the letters I had written from Vietnam — one for each of my 365 days in country, literally a Vietnam journal. During my tour, I had used anything that was available to write home, including a c-ration box top from my breakfast one day. The letters had sat bundled up for years in an old footlocker in the attic under a pile of yard sale "stuff." But, after reading an article about Andrew Carroll and his book *War Letters*, I dragged the footlocker out and took my journey to the next level. Of course, I had known their whereabouts for years; but I had purposely avoided them. Now the letters seemed a natural extension of my poetic efforts. My poetry and letters had combined to become the means to explain, in part, who I am in terms of what I experienced in Vietnam. The resulting manuscript is a glimpse into the inner core of a young soldier at war and how he has changed over the years as told through firsthand accounts written by the young man just hours after actual combat, coupled with intense poems about that combat experience from the same man some thirty years later.

My tour in Vietnam was spent with the 2nd Battalion (Airborne), 506th Infantry Regiment of the 101st Airborne Division. I deployed with the Battalion as the S-1 (Administration Officer), but quickly moved to the line, first as Executive Officer of B Company (Tiger Bravo) and then as its Commander. I finished my tour as Commander of E Company in the same battalion. After all these years, I am surprised and a little embarrassed at the poor grammar in some of the letters. But, in my defense they were often written when I was tired or sleepless, unnerved, lonely or emotionally spent. I can recall many times writing by a red-filtered flashlight at night or scratching out a note on a pickup zone waiting for the next combat assault.

The end result is a book that documents a personal journey of one Vietnam veteran — my own coming of age odyssey, from ingenuous soldier to hardened veteran. Everyone has their own story. I recognize that many veterans of Vietnam, and other wars, experienced more than I did and made greater sacrifices, as well. But, this is my story; take it as just that.

Journey Home

Remembering pieces and catching fleeting glimpses through
a door half open.
No control.
It happens like breathing.

Connecting the pieces takes effort.
Opening the door wider than a crack is difficult.
Turning a glimpse into a stare, hurts.

Fear creeps in.
I slam the door.
Scattering the pieces.
The glimpses vaporize.
Safe again, until next time.

So, it was, from my plane ride home
away from the rice paddies, until now.
Today, I step through the door.
Boldly anticipating the other side.
Eager for the glimpses to reform.

I sit silently
just inside the door.
Transfixed.
Immersed in my visit.
Pieces come together.
A mosaic is formed.

Hello, old friend.
He sits patiently
as if the subject for a portrait painter
unsure of which brush to use.

Soon, I will step away from the door.
Bolder, still.
My long journey home has begun.

IN THE BEGINNING

JUST ARRIVED

During December, 1967, the 101st Airborne Division, except for its 1st Brigade that was already in Vietnam, deployed to "an undisclosed destination in U.S. Army Pacific (USARPAC)" in an operation code-named Eagle Thrust. As part of this deployment I departed the Fort Campbell Army Airfield on December 2nd along with fellow soldiers of the 2nd Battalion (Airborne) 506th Infantry Regiment, leaving behind a 20-year old wife and a six-day old, newborn son. I was the Battalion S1 (Administration Officer) — a young, green 1st Lieutenant just itching to be transferred to a line unit and experience combat. Little did I realize what was in store for me.

December 5, 1967

Phuoc Vinh Base Camp

Well, I'm in base camp. Just about the whole Battalion is up here now. Boy, is it hot! It's 9:30 PM and I'm still sweating. I just finished setting up my room ... used to be a tool shed I think ... I'm tired!

December 6, 1967

Phuoc Vinh Base Camp

Phuoc Vinh is still quiet. Don't worry about me. I sleep at Battalion Headquarters and in my room, I keep a knife, my rifle with six full magazines and two grenades ...

We haven't even started our country training yet. As a matter of fact, we still have two companies left to move from Bien Hoa to Phuoc Vinh — D & A companies ...

December 9, 1967

Phuoc Vinh Base Camp

... I wish that I could make you feel the pride, sense of accomplishment, the honor I feel serving with the 2/506th in the 101st Airborne Division in defense of my country.

... the Colonel told me today that in a couple of weeks I would be going to Bravo Company as the executive officer. . .the Colonel knows I want to go to the line. This is the answer to my dream of 8 long months! I can go back to troops ... I'd better go to bed now. The artillery is playing their nightly lullaby.

December 15, 1967

Phuoc Vinh Base Camp

Last night I went out on an ambush patrol with 1st Inf Div that is manning the perimeter. We went a little way into War Zone D, but didn't catch a thing. Don't worry, I was careful, I was well armed, and I was with professionals. I went with 11 magazines full, 2 frag grenades and a claymore mine. Only 1/2 dozen people in the Bn have been out so far and I am one of them. It really made me feel good to know that I've actually been on a combat patrol.

Was I scared? Yes, but not as much as I thought. I had confidence in myself and I found that the moves that were taught in Ranger School are the moves that were learned by these soldiers in combat. I could even make a determination as to what I liked about the patrol and what I didn't like. Don't you see the advantage I have over other officers and NCO's who are waiting around to be told to go out there? Just remember, everything I do is designed to get me back. I'm in the element that I've spent years being trained for and I'm making decisions that I think are sound and beneficial.

Advice to New Arrivals

Hold hands with the devil.
Kiss your mothers goodbye.
Football and first kisses are illusions.
Only eagles can fly.

Sound the bugles proudly.
Make your lines straight and true.
A bitter life storm is birthing.
The sky is losing its blue.

Lean into the rain and wind.
Lift your faces to the sky.
Close your eyes wide open.
Your salvation is the question why.

March to the sound of battle.
Put your youthful grins aside.
Shoulder to shoulder as brothers.
Do not fear the rising tide.

Listen well to your mother's plea;
your father's son she is trying to save.
That letter with the line at the bottom;
P S. Don't be too brave.

Find the enemy and kill him.
You have only this simple task.
Drive on — drive on — drive on.
That is all your country will ask.

Visit your hearts in the darkest moments.
Feel whenever you dare.
Protect that fertile ground for love to grow,
when you find a life to share.

Search the barren landscape.
Save even a parched, broken dream.
Cherish each rare flowering moment,
nestled by its cool, shady stream.

Fly your guidon fiercely.
Plant it and stake this claim.
A warrior's journey is honorable.
God will remember his name.

And when the guns are hollow echoes,
return home if you can.
Raise your children to hate war,
but revere the warrior man.

On my second night in Vietnam, and first night in Phouc Vinh, I volunteered to go out on ambush with a unit in the 1st Infantry Division that was guarding our perimeter while we became oriented to combat. My battalion in the 101st had not started combat operations yet. I was the Bn S-1 and first one in the battalion to actually go into combat. The next AM — tired, dirty but proud — I had to face an angry Battalion Commander. I guess I should have asked.

Land of Ifs

Dark . . . Black.

You know another soldier is in front of you only because
there has been one a hundred times before, in training.
But, this is different.
It is your first night in Vietnam
and your first ambush patrol.
Too young and inexperienced to be scared.
Just foolish enough to be excited about
 going "outside the wire," before anyone else.

Everyone moves slowly ... carefully.
You're surprised at the quiet chatter among the soldiers.
In Ranger School silence was strictly enforced.
Why are they talking?
What if the VC are listening?
Waiting with their own ambush?
Are the muted voices, really whispers,
signaling your approach?

Pop! ... Shit!
You hear the pop of a trip flare
and the point man's exasperated cry
at making a stupid mistake.
He should have known where it was.
Wasn't he paying attention at the patrol briefing?
You don't remember hitting the ground.

Everyone freezes — some, in midstride.

The flare's white-hot glare flickers, finally goes out.
A friendly booby trap, who would have thought?
The patrol moves again.
Everyone looking for trip wires they can't see in the dark.
Safe again in the blackness.
I guess the VC weren't watching after all.
You have just learned lesson #1:
always expect the unexpected.

Only later, did you think about the ifs.
If, the trip-flare had been a lethal booby trap,
you would have been dead.
If, the VC had been watching and setup their own ambush,
you would have been dead.

Oh well!
Welcome to Vietnam.
Only 363 more nights and 10,000 more ifs to go.

My class from West Point performed magnificently in Vietnam but suffered heavy losses. By the end of the war I had lost 27 classmates killed in action and another 3 from accidents related to combat. Rick Atkinson, the author of *The Long Gray Line: The American Journey of West Point's Class of 1966*, put it this way "By the spring of 1968, most men in the class of '66 were either in country or were preparing to report for duty in the war zone within the next few months ... the class was in the process of amassing nearly a hundred Silver Stars and an even greater number of Purple Hearts, a symbolic tally of valor and shed blood that was far higher than might have been expected of a class of its size ... the death toll continued to rise with monotonous consistency. Soon it proportionately exceeded even the Korean War losses of the class of 1950, a group widely regarded as having been mauled in combat. The chance of being killed in Vietnam was about one in twenty among the '66ers; the chance of being wounded was about one in six."

What Class Are You?

West Point, Class of 1966.

Young men,
like blank canvases,
awaiting the artist's brush.
Fresh eyes, yet to see life,
struggle for a full, panoramic view.

Raging hormones
and blazing energy
clash with old school traditions
and rigid formations.

Hearts broken in romance
soar again with each new adventure.
Friendships start early.
Grow stronger.
Enduring.

A destiny of landing zones
and killing zones.
A terrible price still to pay.
Soon to be

Vietnam, Class of 1968.

FIRST TASTE OF COMBAT

In January of 1968 my request to be transferred to a line unit was granted. I became the Executive Officer of B Company, 2nd Battalion (Airborne) 506th Infantry Regiment — known as Tiger Bravo. Tiger Bravo had just begun combat operations after several weeks of in-country training. On January 16, 1968, we made our very first contact with the enemy. What began as a simple search and destroy operation in War Zone D quickly turned into an all-out fight as we unexpectedly came upon an NVA base camp. Leave it to me to experience one of modern combat's rare events — a bayonet charge — in my very first contact with an armed enemy. The images of that sweltering day in January 1968 are as fresh to me today as they were when I recounted them in these letters home. Some things you just never forget.

January 17, 1968
War Zone D
I haven't written for three days for a very good reason. Tiger Bravo has had its first battle. I am okay, no wounds, no injuries, just tired and in need of a shave ... I was afraid at times but I think I did a creditable job.

We lost 5 KIA (killed in action) and 14 WIA (wounded in action). It was terrible at first. I'll write more about it later tonight but I just wanted you to know that I'm okay ...

They are pulling the company back to Phuoc Vinh for a much-needed rest.

January 17, 1968
War Zone D
Well, am a little settled down now. We should've made at least one or two lines in the newspaper and on TV, that's the reason I wrote that quick first letter. I didn't want you to be worried.

Here's the story. On the morning of the 15th we went on a 1-day operation. We made a helicopter assault into some dry rice paddies

10

and immediately found evidence of Charlie. All that day we found bunker complexes and one Bn size complex of bunkers, tunnels, etc. We found VC graves. We had to dig one up on Col. Mowery's orders. That night we were supposed to come in but the Col. made us link up with Recon platoon (LT Kellogg) who received fire to our south. We linked up with them and spent the night in a tight perimeter. No sleeping rolls, no shaving gear, etc. The next morning after destroying six VC ox carts. We were taking in supplies when the choppers took some sniper shots from 500m away. The company went to investigate. The two lead platoons were caught in a vicious crossfire. We got most of our casualties in the first few seconds. The fire was so intense & the casualties so many that we had to pull back. We had to leave four dead. It hurt all of us to do it but we had to. As the company moved back firing all the time I moved to take charge of the rear elements so that Charlie wouldn't follow us back and hit us again. I brought the Artillery Forward Observer with me and we began to walk the Artillery back as we moved back keeping a blanket of steel between us and Charlie. Shrapnel was falling all around us but it was spent so it didn't hurt anyone. We had to move back 400 meters through the jungle to the landing zone with only one KIA that we could pull out and all our wounded. I had already alerted the medevac choppers as soon as the firing started so they were in the air circling and ready to land. I then took charge of getting the KIA & WIA out and bringing in more ammo, etc.

We then moved right back into the jungle to get our dead. This time we had Delta Company and some armored personnel carriers with us. I was on the left flank when I found three of our dead. We then got attacked again. I ran forward about 10 feet then hit the dirt right next to the fourth body. By this time the CO had given the order to come on line and charge ... there are not many people who have seen or even heard about a bayonet charge in Vietnam but Tiger Bravo did it. The men were great. This second attack the company assaulted yelling and screaming "Airborne, Currahee, etc" shooting, throwing grenades, the whole works. By that time, we had lost about 20% of our people but we were determined to make Charlie pay for what he did to us. We swept through the whole complex blowing tunnels, bunkers, a hospital, everything. Unfortunately, as is the case in most engagements Charlie had gotten out with his bodies. But we know that we got some. When we pulled back the first time he was seen dragging his dead off. This morning we went in a third time but Charlie was gone. So Bn pulled us back to Phuoc Vinh for a rest.

I spent about 2 hours getting our WIA out from the second contact and bringing in supplies for the whole Bn as I was only XO with a radio there...

I've seen the horrors of war and I now can say that I'm a veteran. We earned our CIB's yesterday 10 times over ...

My thoughts have been put down at random and my writing hasn't been too good. I'm tired and I'm still a little numb after all the action. I'm holding my head up very proudly. Tell our son that his father did his job the last couple of days. It was exciting and also very sorrowful and at times sickening but I did it to the best of my ability. This was the first of many engagements probably but it will be the most remembered.

Well, I'm going to close now. The battle is in the past already, it will be long remembered but there are other things coming. We fought well. I hope we continue to do so.

Firefight

Two forces collide.
A chance encounter,
not of lovers or even friends.
Flashes of light from one side
answered by the other.

Close to the ground is the place to be.
A place to stay.
A place to pray.

Speed is all that matters.
Form is for diving competitions.
Fall, flop or fling,
just get down.
Stay down.

In seconds, routine becomes chaos.
Adrenaline pumps.
Hearts pound.
Muscles contract.
Sweat pours.
Mouths become dry.

Sounds creep in.
Ears become baby blues.
Shouts and curses say it all.

Who is alive.
Who is not.
Who is in control.
Who is lost.

Rifle fire speaks as well.
Theirs-ours.
Close-too close.
Each shot its own message,
looking for a recipient.

Soon the flashes of light dim,
flicker,
and go away.
Two forces lurch apart,
reeling as if drunk.

Leaving precious treasures behind.

Some collected in a bag,
for the long journey home.
To be mourned,
put in the ground,
and enshrined on a black V.

Others never recovered,
forever lost.
Leaving holes in hearts and souls,
where innocence once mingled
with feelings and compassion.

In turn,
these wounded hearts and souls
make their way home
to be shoved into dark corners.
Cloaked by despair and guilt.
Chronicled in VA hospital reports.

Or, to be healed by love,
faith and understanding.
Revealed to the sunlight
in one veteran's prose.

First Time/Shadow Eyes

Your walk seems the same,
a little slouchy at first.
There's something about your spirit,
like a balloon that's been burst.

Your voice sounds a little tired,
too low to be you.
No emotion or excitement,
that's got to be a clue.

Something is different,
deep down in your core.
Where you once lived as you,
never the same anymore.

It's the eyes that give you away,
staring past to some other place.
Anywhere but War Zone D,
where death tapped a familiar face.

You've just joined an elite club.
Once in, never out.
A fraternity of young men,
too old to cry or shout.

Just shadow eyes and memories
that stretch past the years.
Coming out in light and dark moments.
Sometimes smiles, sometimes tears.

COWARD'S WAY OUT

There are many ways to avoid combat — some more drastic than others. In this case a soldier went down to the bunker line and took the blasting cap out of a claymore mine, then knelt on it and boom! I can still remember picking up a piece of his shinbone about 2" long as the medics worked at trying to save his leg. There was not much sympathy shown to him as he lay screaming on the ground. Only years later did I stop to think about how frightened he must have been to inflict such a serious wound upon himself.

January 19, 1968

Phuoc Vinh Base Camp

... we had a real punk give himself a self-inflicted wound so that he could get out of the war. He wasn't even with us when we were hit; he's just heard the war stories and got scared. He just came back from AWOL and a few hours later he knelt on a blasting cap and pushed the plunger. Needless to say, he nearly blew his leg off. I think he's a little crazy. But I'll tell you there was little sympathy for him. For one thing, he inflicted this on himself, for another thing he cried, whimpered, screamed; when our wounded who were hit just as bad (didn't) ...

Stops Along the Way

Stops along the way,
especially those that cannot heal,
can make us fragile today,
a little afraid to feel.

Chances not taken
shape who we are, too.
As much as leaps of faith taken
without having a clue.

Messages not heard,
although the voices were clear,
balance sacrifices made
when you hold someone dear.

Memories of the past,
too painful to speak,
become nuggets of truth
for our children to seek.

A stupid choice made,
out of fear in the past,
can be a wakeup call needed
before the die is cast.

It all comes together
in the life that we live.
Troubled or at peace,
we all have something to give.

PARATROOPERS

The airborne community in the 1960's was a small and very proud one. Even in Vietnam, where the concept of parachuting into battle had been replaced by the helicopter, we considered ourselves to be different and members of an elite fraternity of "Paratroopers."

The 2/506th made its last jump at Fort Campbell, Kentucky just weeks before it deployed to Vietnam. Other than one unexecuted plan to jump into Rang Rang, in the center of War Zone D, I never heard of the airborne capability of our battalion being considered for combat operations. But, the rich heritage and traditions of the airborne were a constant source of pride and an integral part of who we were as a fighting unit.

For my part, I reveled in the fact that I was paratrooper in combat with the 101st Airborne Division and participated fully in the airborne mystique. However, I jumped out of perfectly good airplanes while in flight for two reasons. First, I jumped because that's what paratroopers did and still do to this day. Secondly, the extra $110 per month "jump pay" was a bonanza to a 2nd Lieutenant, with a wife and son, whose base salary was only $222 per month.

January 29, 1968
Phuoc Vinh Base Camp
We're holding a Bn Memorial Service tomorrow for our dead. For each paratrooper killed we have a spit shined pair of jump boots, rifle turned upside and jammed into the ground by its fixed bayonet, with a helmet placed on top. It'll be very sad, but along with a firing squad that's the way the airborne honors their dead.

February 18, 1968
Phuoc Vinh Base Camp
For the past four hours, we've had a company band playing in the mess hall on instruments that we've scrounged. We have some real good performers. As I sat there watching the company I couldn't help but compare our troopers with people their own age back in

the states. They are all Mark & Greg's age bracket. They have seen things and done things that I hope Mark & Greg will never experience. Some come from poor homes, rich homes, broken homes. Some are constantly in trouble, others are straight. They're young, they're alive, they enjoy things that Mark & Greg enjoy. But they endured things both physically and mentally that I hope my son will not have to endure. As I look around the room I picked out those who have been wounded, those who have come close, and those who have killed. They have young faces and very old and experienced eyes. They couldn't name the number 1 hit across the nation but they can fire an M-16 with deadly accuracy under constant enemy fire. They haven't eaten a cheeseburger in 3 months but they've gone for long periods without stopping for meals, with very little water in pursuit of Charlie. While others spend nights on dates, studying in libraries or just plain sleeping they've been on ambush patrols, on defensive perimeters, or crouching in foxholes as the whole world erupts around them. Yes, they're the same age as Mark and Greg and given a little time back in the states they could slip right back into the groove. But, there's a difference. They are the legendary "paratroopers." They're members of an elite force. They've put their guts on the line and proven that they are the best of men. They laughed tonight; they had fun tonight but tomorrow they will be paratroopers again — COLD, DEADLY AND TERRIBLY EFFICIENT IN THEIR PROFESSION. The Airborne may be phased out but man will never forget the word "paratrooper."

I just had to put those thoughts down. Sometimes these men drive me crazy, but I can never forget the job they are doing, the sacrifices they're making, the friends they're losing and the chances they're taking. I hope to God that no one in the years to come ever says anything against the "Airborne Soldier" in my presence. In my book, he's the best! Well that's all for now ... I guess I'm in one of my philosophical moods.

Mark and Greg are my two younger brothers. At the time this letter was written they were twenty and eighteen years old respectively. Several months after this last letter was written we began to receive our first "leg", non-airborne qualified, replacements. Before I left Vietnam the 101st Airborne Division was Airborne in name only, we had been officially redesignated as an airmobile division.

Circle of Helmets

"C130 comin' down the strip.
Airborne Daddy gonna take a little trip.
Stand up, hook up, shuffle to the door.
Jump right out and count to four."

Four hundred jungle survivors,
ranks straight, chanting as one.
Guidons leading the way.
Scarred jungle boots kicking up dust.
Marching to say goodbye.

A circle of helmets waits in silence.
No movement or life.
A stillness, known only to the dead.

Rifles with fixed bayonets stabbed into the hard, red clay,
adorned with helmets displaying hard-earned rank.
Pairs of paratrooper's jump boots, like gleaming black mirrors,
complete the ring of airborne tombstones.

One paratrooper memorial,
as simple and stark
as the next.
Rifle – Helmet – Boots.

Rifle – Helmet – Boots.
Rifle – Helmet – Boots.
Until the circle was complete
and War Zone D had spoken.

A trip around the circle,
is a slice of small town Americana.
A tribute to our nation's treasure,
lost on the jungle floor.

A black First Sergeant,
always smiling,
even when denied service at a roadside cafe'
on his way to train troops bound for Vietnam.

A neophyte 2nd Lieutenant,
notorious for getting lost in the jungle.
Doing it one last time, at night,
in front of his own ambush.

A fresh-faced medic,
with dreams of becoming a doctor,
lasting only five seconds
into his first contact with the VC.

Rifle – Helmet – Boots.
Rifle – Helmet – Boots.
Rifle – Helmet – Boots.
Until the circle was complete
and War Zone D had spoken.

Colonel praising the men.
Chaplain saying the prayers.
Honor guard firing the volleys.
Bugler playing the tune.

Leaders remembering the mistakes.
Friends saying the goodbyes.
Everyone staring the stare.

Rifle – Helmet – Boots.
Rifle – Helmet – Boots.
Rifle – Helmet – Boots.
Until the circle was complete
and War Zone D had spoken.

Brothers

In the paddy fields
a line of weary brothers
struggles in the heat.

One hates the boredom
when Charlie is gone
and he has no one to shoot.

One misses his home,
fishing for bass, Jenny's thighs
and cruising downtown.

Another regrets time not spent
holding his children
and loving his wife.

One fears himself,
how he thinks less
about friends lost.

Yet another sees Charlie
all the time,
mostly looking back at him.

But for me,
the long wait for Hell's door to open
is the worst of it.

Decisions Decisions

Travis the Creole walks like a question mark,
back curved under a heavy rucksack,
head and shoulders bent over,
watching as each boot print in front of him
slowly fills with brown paddy water.

His boots doing the same for the one behind.
Part of a file of olive drab ants,
sloshing quietly along
one muddy boot print at a time.

You could tell he is somewhere else,
not here approaching another tree line
with shadows that move and stare back.
Not in this mind-numbing heat,
with lukewarm water seeping into his boots
and coating his feet, already wrinkled and rotting
from days beyond days of cesspool wading.

He is home, before Vietnam and Fort Benning,
remembering the judge's words
said under silver reading glasses,
that kept slipping off his nose.
"Your choice son — hurry up now,
this court is busy."

The voice whirling around under his steel pot
doesn't cut him any slack.

I should have taken the six months!

Six months of probation or three years repairing Army
radios at Fort Monmouth.
What a crock!
I never even saw Monmouth,
just Georgia red clay and black drill sergeants.

I should have taken the six months!

How did I know Suzy stole the beer?
Jumpin in my truck, Yellin — Drive! Drive!
Damn she looked tough.
All sweaty and out of breath.

So, I drove.
Right through a stop sign
in front of the town's only patrol car.
Blue light came on.
Truck got stopped.
Suzy got sent home to grow another year,
and I got the choice.

I should have taken the six months!

FORGOTTEN MEMORIES

TET 68

That Charlie broke the truce over Tet (Vietnamese New Year) didn't surprise any of us. But, the size and ferocity of his attacks did. The United States Air Force Base at Bien Hoa was one of the NVA's primary targets in III Corps. Almost immediately, the 2/506th was plunged into its defense.

Tet hit on our end of month payday. As the Bravo Company Executive Officer, it was my duty to pay the troops. Since we were busy fighting and couldn't stop to be paid, I carried approximately $32,000 in cash (military payment certificates) in my rucksack throughout the battle. I was more worried about losing the money, and making it up on a 1st Lieutenant's salary, than I was about being hit.

January 28, 1968

War Zone D

We're going to be flown to PV in about an hour for the truce. Don't worry we stay just as alert during a truce as not during one. We don't trust Charlie at all even if some other people do ...

January 31, 1968

Phuoc Vinh Base Camp

... you've probably heard of the attacks on Bien Hoa and Saigon. Tiger B was the first company out of Phuoc Vinh into Bien Hoa, I was not with them! x#%**, y*A%##, and x#@l! Maj. Lee had all the XO's stay back because we had to pick up the money to pay the troops today. Well, I picked up the money and paid 17 people, all that remained. B & A Co's killed over 40 VC! B Company so far doesn't even have a WIA and I have to stay here. Maj. Lee makes me so mad! He thinks all XO's should be in base camp ... I feel so useless! If I don't get down there tomorrow I'll go crazy.

... I just found out that Alpha Company had some KIA's. 2LT Galloway was one of them. He was well liked by everyone including me and a fine officer. I'm very sad. Also, a fine NCO who was acting platoon leader and lastly Sgt.E5 Albert E. Coffroth a member of my old platoon. He was a SP/4 then. He was a good soldier. He had volunteered to come to VN because this is his second tour. War is hard but my feelings have not hardened except towards the enemy. No quarter given, no quarter asked. I hope and pray that B Company doesn't lose anyone tonight. Tolette and Mond are going down to Alpha Company tomorrow as platoon leaders because Ronnie D. has only one left — Don Kauffman.

February 2, 1968

Bien Hoa

I know that you've been worried about me because of all the fighting going on near Bien Hoa. Well, I missed the first 24 hours . ..You see they put Tiger B on helicopters at PV and flew them straight to BH. Tiger B was first into the fight, naturally. I got in on the second day of fighting yesterday. Right now, according to Col. Grange, Tiger B is the most famous Co in the Division. We killed over 50 VC while losing 1 KIA and 7 WIA. It's still a steep price, but not bad. The action I got into was all sniper action. We took one section of Bien Hoa and were searching it. All the civilians had pulled out because the NVA (North Viet Army) were in there. We were very considerate of civilian property until we got a man killed and a popular platoon Sgt. seriously wounded. We leveled the place. We can still see the fires off in the distance (we're inside Bien Hoa perimeter now). The wrath of the 101st is terrible but they asked for it. We had tanks, jets the whole works ... The company was as usual magnificent under fire.

February 3, 1968

Bien Hoa

... we're still in Bien Hoa. So far, the Bn count of dead VC is 179. There's talk of getting the Battalion a Distinguished Unit Citation. Gen Barsanti thinks we're great ... I have been recommended for the Bronze Star with V (for valor). I helped evac a couple of wounded under fire and organized a rear defense. I didn't get hurt and it really wasn't as bad as it sounded, but the CO put me in for it ... so things were pretty hot for a while but they've calmed down now.

I Can See It In Your Eyes

You've been there, I know.
I can see it in your eyes.

You've seen it.
Felt it.
Lived through it.

You've wondered how.
Questioned why.
You've been grateful you did survive.

Sometimes,
you feel guilty
that you made it
and your friends didn't.

Sometimes,
as you grow older,
you even think about the VC.
Their dreams cut short.
Their children left behind.
The scars they must carry.

Sometimes,
at the oddest times,
it all comes flooding back.
The sights and sounds
you try to push away.

Yes, my friend
You've been there, I know.
I can see it in your eyes.

COMMAND: A LOVE STORY

During the Vietnam War the U. S. Army established a policy of rotating commanders every 5–6 months. This "revolving door" system had a devastating effect on combat operations — new commanders were prone to make stupid mistakes as they learned about their units, the enemy and themselves. Our Battalion was no exception. During my twelve-month tour in Vietnam I served under three Battalion Commanders and commanded two companies myself.

Command of troops in combat had been a dream of mine since my early days at West Point. I actively sought it and rejoiced when it finally came true. On March 28, 1968 my love affair with B Company (Tiger Bravo), 2nd Battalion (Airborne), 506th Infantry Regiment truly began. I had been the company XO for almost three months and had been in some tough fights with it, but now I was the commander! Only two years after graduating from West Point I was the "old man" and faced with one of the most awesome responsibilities of my life.

March 28, 1968

Phuoc Vinh Base Camp

Today I assumed command of B Company (Tiger Bravo), 2nd Battalion (Airborne), 506th Infantry ... today I am a proud man.

Maj Boyd and just about every officer, NCO and EM shook my hand. My men have confidence in me. They've told me so, but even more I can feel it. We had a party today and the 1st Sgt made an announcement that Tiger B was getting a new CO. He said some very nice things about me and then he said my name and I walked up to say a few words . ..They cheered! I feel so good ... they cheered.

Tomorrow I take the company to the rocket belt to chase Charlie, I can do it. I know I can ... I can't lose.

April 12, 1968

Fire Support Base (FSB) Concord

You asked if being CO was lonelier. Yes, it is. The responsibility is much, much greater than anything I have ever had. But, I welcome it. This is my profession.

May 25, 1968

Phuoc Vinh Base Camp

...I have found that as a company commander I have to be strong! If I falter then the company loses something intangible and people will die unnecessarily for it. I can't unbend for a second in Vietnam- ...I've had to be harsh sometimes and completely unwavering at other times. Usually my troopers don't realize the good that I'm doing for them (My constant harping on security, my sometimes hard but always swift execution of discipline). I have to do it. These men have been entrusted to me and it's my duty to give them my all.

Don't get me wrong I can honestly say that I'm a popular commander and that my troopers have excellent morale. I guess that I've been able to mix the proper amounts of discipline, wisecracking and a show of interest on my part to keep this company a tight, yet happy fighting unit.

I've never had a man killed while under my command but I know it will come. I have had many wounded, some are back in the states, and some have returned to the company already.

August 27, 1968

Phuoc Vinh Base Camp

Well, Tiger B is no longer mine. I'm still glad I'm off the line and I wouldn't go back if given a choice; but there was just something about getting on a chopper today and leaving Bravo Company. I've been through a lot with Tiger B. The things that I've done and seen will stay with me for a long time. There is something about sharing hardships, dangers and sorrows that forms a tie that is hard to break. I was their commander, the "old man", who saw them laugh, cry, die, bleed, and even heard some screams. I know which men are brave, which have too much fear in them to ever control. I know the good and the bad. I've felt all their emotions, many times much deeper than them. I've given orders and made decisions knowing that someone might not come back; but I know in my heart that I did everything within my power to do my job as the company commander to see that any operation would be a success. They were mine! There is something awesome about engaging the enemy in battle. I've done it quite a few times and I know that Tiger B could fight. They are the best. They are the American fighting man and I've had the privilege of leading them in their ultimate destination — BATTLE. I'm proud, and I always will be, of Tiger Bravo.

I guess I'm a little sad tonight, huh?

The very next day Tiger Bravo, under their new commander, my good friend Terry Van Meter, was ambushed near Trang Bang and suffered heavy casualties. I was still at our Base Camp preparing to take over another company when the first reports came in. I was devastated upon hearing the news.

August 29, 1968

Phuoc Vinh Base Camp

Well, the fighting still goes on near Trang Bang. Terry was shot twice in the chest with one of the rounds coming out his neck. However, he is doing OK and is now in a hospital in Long Binh. Our S-4 Frank Casey went to visit him and said that he was talking and smiling. So don't feel bad, he's OK.

I don't know who has Tiger B. They haven't called for me so I imagine they've found someone. I'm glad and sad. Do you understand? Tiger B lost two men killed last night. One of them was SSG Lamb 15 on your list. I'm glad that I'm off the line but I'm sad that I can't help Tiger B like I could when I was the CO. I've been through a lot with them and it hurts me to see them get hit without me. Do you understand? I really can't understand it myself.

After six months as a rifle company commander in the 101st Airborne Division I went on Rest and Recuperation (R&R) to Hawaii for seven days. Upon my return, I was promised a job on the Battalion Staff as the Intelligence Officer. But several hours off the plane from Hawaii I was told that my old company (Tiger Bravo) was in a terrible ambush. I was ordered to go back and take command. In the ambush, I lost a very close friend — 1LT Joe Hillman (Call sign Tiger Bravo 16). This poem tells the story of my return to Tiger Bravo.

Just Another 24 Hours

Off the line and happy,
I've done my part.
A job at headquarters
about to start.

An ambush is sprung,
like so many before today.
"Your old unit is in trouble."
A messenger stops to say.

Chopper is on the way
to bring you back.
Rifle, helmet
and that damned rucksack.

Briefing at Brigade,
I hurry up to sit.
Whisper from a friend,
"B Company has hit a lot of shit."

Chopper lifts off.
It's getting dark already.
More briefings in the air.
Hands not too steady.

Night is now all black
except for a pretty ring of light.
Pretty my ass!
It's a huge firefight.

Radio on speaker.
I hear voices and sounds of a fight.
"Someone help us.
Don't think we'll make it through this night."

"Put me down anywhere.
I'll crawl back to that ring of light
Those are my men
That's my company in this fight."

"Too dangerous! It's suicide.
You'll be killed," they all say.
Who cares? I want to be with my men
to help them see the next day.

Chopper heads home,
away from the light.
Leaving my men and their fears
to face that damned night.

Reinforcements aren't around.
Artillery and air strikes will be there still.
But I won't be on the ground
to add my meager skill.

Next day I'm back.
Charlie seems gone.
Let's see what's left
this miserable dawn.

Bodies are still in the killing zone.
It's easy to see.
I grab a medic and say,
"Stick close to me."

I'm looking for those alive,
and a special one you see.
He is Tiger Bravo 16,
A good friend to me.

I know he was one
that Charlie could never claim.
But, I listened all night for his voice
that never came.

I find him up front,
hoping he's not dead.
But, this is Vietnam.
He took one in the head.

I can count my good friends
on one hand, as they say.
I've just lost one finger
and feel no pain this terrible day.

The pain tries to come
but I know what to do.
Push it down deep
where it can't get to you.

The day is now full.
More dead I must face.
Just another 24 hours
in this hard, cruel place.

Take Me Now

Take me now!
I have passed all your tests.

When SGT P. was hit in the alley during Tet,
I pulled him out.
When LT T's platoon was decimated
that terrible summer night,
I walked point through the firefight,
linking up with the pieces in that clearing.

I have been there each time.
You know I have.

But, if your plan is for me to fail the next time,
or the time after that,
or even the very last time on my tour.
To let my soldiers down.
To cost them their lives for mine.
Then take me now.

Take me now!

WOUNDED IN ACTION

Exactly six months to the day I arrived in Vietnam my luck ran out. I was one of 4,308 casualties during the first week of June — the 438 KIA and 3,870 WIA amounted to the highest weekly total to date in the war.

The 2/506th had been deployed to the Central Highlands to support the 4th Infantry Division. The move was so secret that we had to take our 101st patches off our uniforms and adhere to strict radio silence. Bravo Company was sent to a Fire Support Base west of Dak To to reinforce a battalion from the 4th Infantry Division that had been hit very hard the night before. The Battalion Commander, LTC Mike Malone, had been one of my leadership instructors at West Point. He was elated to have an Airborne company to help out. The day after our arrival he sent my company across the valley floor to look for the NVA that had almost overrun his base two nights before. Well, I found them and the rest, as they say, is history.

I spent three weeks recovering from my wounds, then returned to my beloved Tiger Bravo.

June 2, 1968
Pleiku Evacuation Hospital
Well, I've been in Vietnam for 6 months today and I went and did it. I'm in the hospital with a minor shrapnel wound in the back. I am all right ... I'm safe and sound in the hospital at Pleiku ... I 'll be moved to a hospital in Cam Ranh Bay tomorrow or the next day ... the shrapnel didn't hit anything except a little ole muscle and they took it right out. Very little pain when I got hit

You should be proud ... Tiger B beat Charlie but good. I had 10 slightly wounded and 1 serious case (he's ok now) and we killed 10 NVA confirmed, maybe 10 others and arty got 6–8. I'm so proud of my men.

June 3, 1968

Pleiku Evacuation Hospital

I was working with the 4th Infantry Division out of a fire support base west of Dak To. On the morning of the 2nd my company was given the mission of sweeping a couple of kilometers to the north and then back into the FSB. We saw signs of fresh activity about 1 kilometer out. About 1400 we found a bunker complex that had been built in the last few days and used in the last few hours. We even found fresh chow half-eaten. So, I spent a couple of hours very carefully checking the area. It was getting late about 1600 when I decided to move back to the FSB. I had to make it back before dark because we traveled light and weren't supposed to spend the night (under orders). Also, the FSB needed my company there at night or they'd probably get overrun.

As we moved out from the base camp area we came across cache points with a couple of weapons, ammo, etc in them. This instantly put me on full alert. I moved the 2nd platoon to the cache points (I only had the 2nd, 3rd, and 4th plts with me, 1st platoon was detached to guard a couple of bridges). Well, Charlie was in the cache points. My point man killed the first Charlie outright. He got hit with 2 full magazines from 2 different people. Since we were receiving fire the 2nd platoon continued to pour fire into the area. My first two casualties came from 1) one of my men with a grenade launcher shot too close to one of his buddies and a small fragment hit him in the foot (very minor). 2) PFC Limer who is Palagyi's ass't went up forward to see what was going on and as the case when you're in an area you aren't supposed to be you get hurt. He got shot 4 times. But he's not even in serious condition in the hospital here. I saw him last night (He's the worst WIA). Then I pulled the 2nd Plt back a little way and let Joe Palagyi call in arty for about 30 minutes. We had to get the wounded out so my 1st Sgt and the 3rd Plt as security went 100m to the west to bring in dustoff. That left me with the 2nd and 4th Plts right on the edge of what we think is a huge cache area. In the 4 bunkers that were in our little area (Charlie was in the rest) we found 1 machine gun, 1 AK-47, 1 SKS carbine and 2 75mm recoilless rifles (they're big). After the artillery worked over Charlie for a while I moved in with the 2nd Plt going on the left (with me) 4th Plt on the right. Then all hell broke loose. It was the 2nd Plt up against a Plt of NVA. They were using AK-47's, light machine guns, RPG (rocket launchers) and grenades to begin with. Well, there we were; 2 Plts slugging it out! My 2nd Plt killed 10 NVA right off the bat without taking any casualties. I was right up there with the Plt Leader PSG Sykes. Then Charlie hit us with his big stuff. He hit us with 82mm & 60mm mortars. In a few seconds, the whole area that the 2nd Plt was in erupted in about 25 seconds of pure hell. Myself and 8 others were hit. There was nothing I could do but pull my people out of there back to the LZ where the 3rd Plt was and let Palagyi call in the world on Charlie (which he did). Also, it was getting extremely late and we had to break contact so we could get back before dark.

I was hit at 1700 hours. I was with PSG Sykes facing the gooks when the mortars went off to my left rear. The frag is only 1/2-inch-long but it knocked me head over heels. It never really bothered me though. I had a company to run and a little old frag wasn't going to stop me.

Well, I was dusted off — last one — from the field. It hurt to leave Tiger B. I should be back in the Bn in a couple of weeks though and maybe I'll get it back. I'm so proud of my men. We beat Charlie without getting anyone killed.

... my WIA's were just great. No cries, no whimpers just wise cracks and tight smiles through clinched teeth. My men are paratroopers all the way. Limer who had been shot 4 times was lying in the dirt with 2 medics working on him when I walked up and said, "How's it going Clem (his nickname)." He looked up at me and said something very simple, "It hurts sir!" Then he went back to staring at the sky and clinching his teeth...one of my medics was hit also. They always get hit because they are always there; it's as easy as that.

June 4, 1968
Cam Ranh Bay
I'm now at the 6th Convalescent Center in Cam Ranh Bay. I hope that I won't be here long ...I go to see my doctor tomorrow to get the final word ... this place is right on the beach (I can't go in the water), has hot showers (I can't take a shower), has a snack bar, movies, library, PX, USO show ...

... none of the tension has left me yet. I guess it will if I stay here any length of time. I just can't get over the fact that myself nor anyone else is walking around without a weapon. It has become a part of me the last six months and I just can't get used to it.

Purple Hearts

Scars on bodies.
Cuts on souls.
Purple hearts and reunions,
try to cover the holes.

Scars fade.
Memories remain.
Souls heal,
but not the pain.

License plates on cars.
Purple hearts in drawers.
No talk of the scars.
Memories behind doors.

Children don't ask.
Talk not an option.
It's easier to avoid,
than to risk explanation.

A ROUGH 10 DAYS

Adversity makes one stronger. If that is true, then I came out of the summer of 1968 a very strong man. It seemed like we were always in contact, ranging from minor actions such as snipers and booby traps to major engagements with NVA Battalions. There were many tough times that summer, but this particular period was one when my morale just about bottomed out. The weight of command and constant losses had taken their toll.

July 25, 1968
Vicinity of Cu Chi

I'm back out in the field now still working for 1/506th. The 2/506th is down here now but we haven't gone back under their control. We've had light contact all day long. I've had one casualty. A new LT (Jim Cress) got shot in the leg.

Well in the last 30 minutes a lot has happened. We've made contact again and 2/506th has taken over command of us again.

I'm wet, lonely and miserable. I don't want to be out here.

July 25, 1968
Vicinity of Cu Chi

... we were put back under control of 1/506th. We have 8 companies surrounding a Bn. Last night we were put in here and told to go to the aid of a platoon from A/2/506th who were surrounded. It took 4 hours and I lost 2 good men killed before we got to them. PSG Tellis was one of my killed. This morning I lost another man killed when he tried to get a gook out of a tunnel but the gook got him.

... why must people die in this miserable country? A Company had LT Tolette and LT Williams killed yesterday. I wish I could be kind and gentle in breaking the news but I'm so sick of the blood and death I've seen. PSG Tellis was killed just 10 minutes after I had given the order to him to move his platoon to the front and start moving. This is a hard and dirty type of fighting with Charlie behind every hedgerow ... I can't take it anymore. Honest, I just can't take more of my men getting killed and wounded. I'm not saying this lightly, I've just had too much.

... I've been in contact for 2 days and haven't slept in 2 days.

July 27, 1968

Vicinity Cu Chi

... we got lifted out of the battle site at 1530 yesterday because Charlie broke contact. We went straight into a combat assault north of Cu Chi. I got the company up at 0200 this morning because I had to be in position around a village at 0600. C, D & B Companies are surrounding this village with A Company searching it. A Company already had 4 or 5 casualties from booby traps and I have two. PSG Sykes was one of my wounded (both of mine are wounded). One was bad and Sykes wasn't too bad off.

... I still feel the same way. I want to get off the line. I'm tired of this war. Just so tired.

... the realization of what could happen has finally caught up with me.

July 28, 1968

Vicinity of Cu Chi

Well, last night I took 3 more casualties from a booby trap. I've just about had it. The only thing that keeps me going is ... the duty concept that West Point beat into me. That won't let me quit. My company is down to 82 people. I used to have 4 Plts but because I have lost so many people and leaders I have dropped to 3 Plts and they're all at half strength. This is the notorious dirty "nickel & dime stuff that the VC are good at (nickel & dime meaning 2 or 3 casualties at a time).

Thank God, I can hide my feelings and keep a stone face. Otherwise everyone would know how I feel...like I said I still have my duty concept to keep me going so my efficiency as a CO hasn't been touched but I'm all torn up inside. I won't ever be lax or fall to pieces, but I just want out.

... I hope I don't have more casualties today. They hit me very deeply in my heart when I see my people loaded on choppers killed or wounded.

July 29, 1968
Vicinity of Cu Chi
I took two more casualties yesterday afternoon. We were lifted out of an open field by helicopter and two of my men were hit by sniper fire just as the choppers lifted off the ground. That aircraft went straight to the hospital. When we landed about 5 kilometers away the gunships escorting us received heavy automatic weapons fire from a canal, 200 meters to the east of the LZ. I called in artillery and two jets. Then we swept through the area but found nothing.

Last night we set up in rice paddies. Just about everything was under water. Right now, we're on a little island of dry land in the middle of rice paddies ...

July 30, 1968
Vicinity of Cu Chi
No casualties yesterday ... things look a little brighter now ... one minor casualty today, a man from Recon Platoon (attached to me) fell into a punji pit and got one in the leg.

... you can probably tell from this letter that I'm getting out of my mood. It'll stay with me I know because it isn't actually a mood but the truth.

July 31, 1968
Cu Chi Base Camp
We came back into Cu Chi to rest and repair equipment for a day. We'll be going back out tomorrow. I took 2 more wounded this morning when we had some light contact coming back in. We set up in dry rice paddies last night then it started raining and by midnight there was a foot of water everywhere. Miserable! I kept dry all night

with a poncho until 0830 this morning when a sniper opened up and a couple of RPG's (rockets) were fired at us. I dove into about six inches of paddy water (really miserable). I just received word that one of my wounded of 3 or 4 days ago lost his leg on the operating table. I'll have to visit him tomorrow.

I'm just about completely out of my depressed state. I know that I have a job to do and no matter how bad it gets I owe it to ... the country and Tiger B to stick it out as long as I'm told to.

August 1, 1968
Cu Chi Base Camp
Last night I visited some of my wounded in the hospital. One of them had lost his right leg but he was in real good spirits. He was a booby trap victim. Since we were in Cu Chi I had my people on sick call. Four were put into the hospital outright and about six others were given light duty from sickness, disease, etc.

... also I saw PSG Sykes. He'll stay in Nam but he won't walk for about two months.

... everyone is in real good spirits.

Well, we'll be going back out today. The time will pass but not fast enough.

August 2-3, 1968
Vicinity of Cu Chi
... I had a big contact last night and today. We hit estimated platoon of VC and they threw in mortars just like at Dak To. I had 14 wounded total, only 11 of which needed to be evaced and 5 of these 11 were treated and released. This morning we hit the same group with no casualties. I held up and called in 3 air strikes and over 2,000 rounds of artillery. C Company is sweeping through the area now but they probably won't find anything. The VC are great at disappearing. I received 11 brand new replacements yesterday at 1700 and at 2300 I had 11 wounded evaced. I'm just not making any headway.

... chopper coming in.

Unimaginable

Unimaginable.
Is how you described your first time in combat.
Fear and excitement all mixed together.
Instant chaos of jumbled sounds, movement and emotions.
Helmet falling off when you hit the ground.
Feeling the sting of sweat running into your eyes.
A shower of leaves filtering down from the bullets striking
branches above your head.
Freezing up!
Then talking yourself through what you needed to do.
Pushing fear away.
Never knowing where it went or what made it go.

Unspeakable.
Is how many of your friends reacted to the worst of that
endless year.
Never speaking.
Never sharing.
Trying to put it all behind and get on with life.
Placing images of poncho wrapped bodies, dead friends and
destroyed villages
on a shelf in the back of the store where stock clerks
never visit.
Wrapping still simmering emotions of naked rage and
profound grief
in a protective coating of lead before sinking them to the
bottom of the sea.
But, speak of it you did!
Writing letters of battles lost and won.
Carefully sanitized and pasteurized for home consumption.
And, speak of it you did!

Taking pen in hand and writing about forgotten memories
and all too real aftermaths and aftershocks.
Swapping your tales with other vets screaming silently to
tell someone—anyone.
And, speak of it you did!
Revealing deep scars by the glow of candles with your
special love.

Uncomfortable.
Is how you felt the first few years back.
Wondering why you made it and not the others.
Reflecting on your time in country and your countless life
and death decisions.
Learning how to feel again and open up—even if just a little.
Getting to know your almost toddler son,
who you knew mainly through letters and photographs.
Waiting for a welcome home parade,
but finding Main Street preoccupied with the war,
not the warriors.
Realizing that the protesters were right all along,
we never should have been there.
That dominos were just harmless ivory pieces and not a
geo-political theory.
Feeling ashamed that it took years to admit it publicly.

Unbelievable.
Is how you describe your luck over the past thirty years.
Finding a woman who loves you—forgotten memories and all.
Realizing that a relationship is a work in progress.
Sometimes celebrating milestones with champagne and
ribbon cutting,
while other times handing out hard hats to anyone within
ear shot.

Remembering those times she changes TV channels from a
war movie,
hoping you won't notice.
But you do without letting on and loving her for it.
Raising great kids with kid's problems, but your values.
Enjoying a career highlighted by friendships made and
sacrifices shared,
rather than opportunities squandered and integrity eroded.

Unshakable.
Is how you characterize your belief in a loving and caring God.
Even in the darkness of that year—a small light glowed.
Sometimes dim.
Sometimes flickering.
But, never extinguished!
Finding peace in the early years just sitting in church.
Remembering how great it felt the first time
that peaceful feeling stayed with you as you walked
out the door.
But nothing like the one that awaits you in the next life
where the joys will truly be

Unimaginable.

It Doesn't Hurt to Ask

Jesus,
help me make it through this fight.
I don't think I can grip this rifle more tight.
Please, don't let me out of your sight.
Stay with me in this hole the rest of the night.
Thanks.

HAPPY BIRTHDAY

Ground combat of any era is a young man's war and Vietnam was no exception. I had lived ten lifetimes before my 24th birthday. The very next day the battle was carried in the Stars and Stripes — our official newspaper in Vietnam.

August 6, 1968

Vicinity Cu Chi

Well, I'm 24! We didn't get to a fire support base last night. We went straight into another battle. Luckily, we didn't see any action. A Company did and Matt has been wounded. He's not serious because I heard him on the radio a couple of hours after he was hit. What a birthday party. The sky was lit up by flares, tracers everywhere, air strikes, etc. I was up all night and right about midnight the battle was still going on. The gooks were shooting anti-aircraft fire at helicopters, jets, anything ... the body count for the action on the 25th is not 78 gooks Today's (actually last night's) is 16 so far.

Place Without Angels

I have been to a place without angels,
where miracles are measured in days alive.
Grace is only a word
in someone else's vocabulary.

Where the primitive beauty of the land
is lost to a soldier's eye.
Replaced by circles, on a map,
of VC controlled areas or likely ambush sites.

Where a gentle people are friend today
and a deadly foe tomorrow.
Or, is it foe, then friend?

Where young Americans and Vietnamese
are caught in the same ancient ritual.
A war conceived by the elders
and fought by the sons.
One, as far from being an imperialist
as the other is from being a communist.

Where friends lost and battles won live again,
years later.
In a secret place in my mind.
Where today becomes the memory
 and back then becomes today.

Where release comes from writing prose
in a cigar bar, 4,000 miles from home
and thirty years from the battlefield.

But, deep down, still
in a place without angels.

SGT NAP

The losses in Vietnam were hard on everyone, especially the families left behind who often never learned the details of their loved ones' death. Here is an exchange of letters between a recent widow and me, asking how her husband died.

The soldier was PSG Tellis. He was an extremely popular NCO who the troops affectionately call "Sgt. NAP." In those days, we began to receive replacements that were non-airborne personnel or NAP for short. Our company rosters even annotated who was non-airborne by including "NAP" by their name. PSG Tellis was the highest-ranking non-airborne personnel in the company. While the term "NAP" was used in a derogatory fashion by some paratroopers, in the case of PSG Tellis it was just the opposite. His nickname was given to him as a measure of the troops' respect and admiration. He was just the type of person you liked and looked up to — a real leader! Everyone knew and respected Sgt. NAP!

August 9, 1968
Old Hickory, Tennessee

Dear Sir,
This is to inform you that today I mailed a box of canned foods that I had previously mailed to my dear husband that was in your Company, but it was returned to me on the 8th of August because my husband SCF William J. Tellis (RA16293259) was killed on July 26, 1968 at Cu Chi, Vietnam.

My desire is for you to distribute the contents of the box to the troops in his Battalion as you see fit. I hope it will make them happy as I knew it would if my husband had received it.

Would you write me and give the cause of his death? It was a sudden shock to me and it's really hard to understand what happened to him. His last letter was written to me on July 24, and he was killed on 26 July. I hope the troops enjoy the snacks.

Sincerely,
Mrs. William J. Tellis

August 21, 1968

Location Unknown

Dear Mrs. Tellis,

I'm very sorry that I haven't written sooner, but I could not write without knowing if you had been notified of your husband's death. Please accept my sympathies and those of the men of Tiger Bravo on your loss. Being his company commander during the battle in which he lost his life, I can truly say that I am sorry from the bottom of my heart.

Your gift of the box of food will be greatly appreciated by the men who served with your husband. Knowing how fine a man he was, I am sure that he would want it this way. The action in which your husband gave up his life was centered around a platoon from A Company that had been cut off, surrounded, and all of it leaders killed by the enemy. It was B Company's mission to go to the aid of the surrounded platoon. Your husband was killed by a sniper's bullet while we were forcing our way through the enemy surrounding the platoon. Your husband's actions prior to his death warranted me to submit his name to the Battalion Headquarters for an award for valor in action. I feel it will help you to know that after four hours B Company finally broke through and saved thirty American lives. Unfortunately, I lost two more brave soldiers in the attempt.

Mrs. Tellis, I am not quite capable of expressing the depths of my feelings on paper. As a company commander, I have the ultimate responsibility for the lives of my men and I die a little for each one I lose. I promise you one thing — I have a son who is 8 ½ months old — I promise that he will grow up knowing that men such as your husband gave up their lives so that he might be free. Again, please accept my sympathies.

Respectfully,

Richard St John

Commanding

We tried twice that night to reach the platoon from A Company that was surrounded. PSG Tellis was killed on the first attempt. After we pulled his body back we tried again. This time I took the lead. It was the only time in Vietnam when I knew I was going to die! But, I didn't. I survived to write his widow a month later and to pen this poem over thirty years after that.

Lost Forever

Think of their minds and what they could have discovered.
Their hands and what they could have built.
Their hearts and how they could have loved.
Their compassion and whom they could have touched.

Now they are 58,000 names on a V in a marble city.
Not forgotten, but barely remembered.
Holidays and birthdays and history lessons bring them
to life.
Most days they are just names on a wall.
Looked at, photographed, sometimes touched — but always
walked by.

What if among them was a Salk or Edison or
Hemmingway?
Cancer would be a memory, not a curse.
Jordan would be a good one, but a truly great one would
have soared higher.
Novels would be on the shelves and songs sung on
Broadway.
Billions would be made on Wall Street and souls saved on
Main Street.
Bomber McVeigh may have been stopped before the yellow
truck was parked.

But most of all,
and best of all,
little girls would have a Daddy to hug.
Little boys would have someone to catch their very first
curve ball.

What if they had all come back?

A DANGEROUS PLACE

Ground combat in Vietnam was a chaotic and contradictory environment of ubiquitous, indiscriminate danger interspersed with boring, mind-numbing days and nights. It played out against a backdrop of quiet, serene beauty that one would expect to find in a backward, Southeast Asia country. The secret to survival was to neither dwell on the beauty nor succumb to the boredom; but to be constantly on the edge — always searching for the new face that danger would present. It could come at any time and in many forms.

I distinctly remember one incident that never made it into a letter home. My company was setup in a perimeter a long way from anywhere in the middle of VC country when a cobra rose up from a small bamboo thicket inside the perimeter. Immediately, several soldiers started shooting at what was now an equally frightened snake. Soon others joined in the shooting. Picture this — a circle of soldiers, probably 50 meters in diameter, firing wildly in towards the center. Now that was a dangerous place! Luckily no one, except the cobra, was injured.

January 4, 1968
Phuoc Vinh Base Camp
Ron Nelson was injured by a grenade today. He and three others went into a shell crater where there was a dud grenade ... I don't know what he was thinking about because you never — NEVER — mess around with duds. Well, the grenade went off. All four were wounded but none critically. Ron has burns on his right arm and multiple fragments in his hands and lower legs. The first report is that he'll be out of action for 3 or 4 weeks but then come back to the Bn. Don't worry I have more sense than him.

February 14, 1968
Phuoc Vinh Base Camp
Phuoc Vinh was mortared last night. All the rounds landed towards the center of Phuoc Vinh outside our Bn area. It was late at night but I

couldn't sleep. I heard them fired and I heard them on impact. No big thing; I went back to sleep.

March 16, 1968

Phuoc Vinh Base Camp

Quite an exciting night last night. There was an outdoor movie being shown at Bn Hqs. Tom Eller and I went. Charlie threw a mortar round in about 100 meters away. Needless to say, the show was postponed for about 20 minutes. He mortared again later on. No injuries in the Bn.

March 19, 1968

War Zone D

You're probably worried because you have probably heard of a paratrooper unit getting hit hard near Phuoc Vinh. It was the 3/187th not us. We were only 6 clicks away but saw nothing. So far, they have 25 KIA and 56 WIA. I don't know how many enemy but I hope it was a lot for the price they paid.

April 8 & 18, 1968

Rocket Belt (North of Bien Hoa)

I have some very sad news. CPT Whitehead was killed yesterday in an accident. He was walking towards a helicopter and was hit in the head with the blade. He lived for only 1 hour. Everyone took his death hard, just as I know you are. Being around helicopters is dangerous but I always keep bending over low. I'm sorry that I can't be there to comfort you ... God will look after us

He was walking towards a helicopter that LT Mond was getting out of. He had his steel pot on. He was just about halfway through his salute when the blade hit him in the eyes. The motor of the helicopter was turned off. Whenever a motor is turned off the blades still rotate like a fan and as they go slower they dip down because of the weight. He was on a high spot and the chopper was on a low spot. He lived for 1 hour but said nothing.

April 15, 1968

Rocket Belt (North of Bien Hoa)

One of Mac's ambushes that he sent out from PV got ambushed instead. One of the men died. Charlie company went all that time with no action, now they're getting it in lumps.

April 26, 1968

Rocket Belt (North of Bien Hoa)

My company got hit by lightning last night. We were knee deep in rice paddies during a storm and wham! It knocked over 7 people and 2 of them were bad enough to evac.

They're all right though. Did I tell you about the man who got butted by a water buffalo 2 or 3 days ago? He got evaced too. We had to kill the buffalo or he would've killed my man.

May 3, 1968

Rocket Belt (North of Bien Hoa)

Yesterday we got word that a man in Tiger B has malaria. That's pretty good considering we've been in country for 5 months. I think it's the first in the Bn.

... the medics just came up and gave me my malaria pill. Little white "Dopson" every day and a big orange one every Monday.

May 9, 1968

Rocket Belt (North of Bien Hoa)

Yesterday Ron Darnell lost 4 KIA and 6 or 7 WIA, most lost limbs, to a command detonated claymore mine on a trail ...! There's been quite a bit of activity in the rocket belt lately, one of my platoons is out right now and thinks he is being followed. He is setting up a hasty ambush to see what he can catch. He might pull it off, but I have my doubts because Charlie is slick.

May 30, 1968

Rocket Belt (North of Bien Hoa)

Ronnie Darnell shot himself in the foot while cleaning his weapon. It's not serious but will require hospitalization. He hurt his pride more than his foot.

August 23, 1968

War Zone D

I'm sorry I didn't write yesterday, but I was moving all the way to dark. We started out going north from the FSB about 2 ½ kilometers and we ran into some NVA. I had one man slightly wounded and no enemy. At the same time, we were getting hit from the front I got hit from the rear. Lo and behold it turned out to be an ARVN company (supposedly friendly). Luckily, they can't hit the broad side of a barn so I didn't take any casualties. The S-3 canceled that operation and made me walk 7 ½ kilometers to get away from our numbskull allies.

October 4, 1968

Camp Eagle (I Corps)

It is cold at night. Really, it's just like Dak To. Camp Eagle got rocketed last night. I was in a ditch watching them hit farther in. It was pretty spectacular.

Images of Butterflies

Time and motion slow.
Sounds fade.
A constant search for danger gives way.
Replaced by a brief moment
of soft images and snatches of color.

Green jungle wrapped in shimmering white heat.
A cool breeze from nowhere, just as I seek shade.
A trail bending to the left at the top of the hill
disappears into a tunnel of bamboo.

Radios silent.
No static crackling or voices reporting.
The ache in my shoulders gone.
My rucksack forgotten.
At the top of the hill — butterflies!
Dozens of yellow butterflies silently fluttering into view.
It is a golden moment.
Just as silently — three small, black figures
move gracefully amidst the butterflies into the dark tunnel.

I stare.
Not moving.
Not drawing a breath.
Savoring the images for what they are,
an escape into a moment of beauty and tranquility.

But reality is not about to lose this fight.
It quickly regains its hold.
I remember why we are watching the trail.
The black figures are not performing a ballet;
they are my prey.

Butterflies are only a backdrop
to the drama that must now unfold.
Shots chase the black figures down the tunnel.
Yellow butterflies scatter.

The moment passes as quickly as it had come,
but the images of butterflies remain.

Slackman and Riley

A deafening sound—hot air slaps them around.
A shower of dirt, leaves and scraps of cloth follows.
Riley's body jackknifes across a rotten log,
More red, than olive drab.

> *"What the hell happened?*
> *"Booby trap — here take my rifle."*
> *"Cut away his pants — shit, what a mess!"*
> *"Got to stop the bleeding."*

A hand reaches up, another reaches down.
Two buddies hold tight to each other.
Frantic efforts and cursing voices fade away.
A low voice speaks, not yet a whisper.

"Slackman, are you there?"   *"Yeh, Riley, I'm here."*
"My foot?"   *"Yeh, Riley, it's your foot."*
"Where is it?"   *"I don't know."*
"Find it! I WANT MY FOOT!"   *"OK! OK! Lay back*
— just lay back."

More help arrives, with more staring eyes.
Sergeant Dee, bleeding from his nose and ears,
pushes past the new guy from Kentucky.

> *"Grab his arms; get him off this log."*
> *"Shit — look at his back!"*
> *"Shut up, Goddamn it!"*
> *"Stuff your towel in the hole."*
> *"Keep pressure on it."*
> *"Where's the medic?" "Anyone seen Doc?"*

The two buddies talk.
Relaxed and easy,
like they were sitting on the bunker line at base camp,
bullshitting about nothing,
while passing a beer back and forth.
Take a swig — wipe the bottle off — pass it on.

"Is it bad Slackman?"   "Riley-damn your ass-yes, it's bad."
"Huh — how come I don't hurt much?"   "I don't know
                                            shock I guess."
"Water — I'm thirsty man."   "Here, my canteen still
                                    has some koolaid in it."
"That's good, thanks — save some for later."   "OK."

Slackman checks into the real world.
Training fights off emotion.
This is a race.
Everyone knows it — even Riley.

                                    "Where's Doc?
                "Workin on Smitty — said give him a minute."
                                "CO call medevac?"
                        "Yeh — ten minutes ETA."
                                    "Damn!"

Nothing else matters now.
The two buddies sense the same thing.
They are at the center of their own universe.
No outsiders allowed.
No time to say goodbye.

"Slackman?"   *"Yeh."*
"Everything's getting dark, what's happening?'   *"Nothing*
                         Riley, you've just lost a lot of blood."
Silence.   *"Riley! Riley! Hang on, buddy!"*
Silence.   *"Damn your ass-don't you die on me!"*
Silence.

Doc showed up two minutes later,
IV in hand — ready to stick.
Medevac came in seven minutes, not ten.
Riley's right foot was found in a tree.
It went in his body bag.
As for Slackman,
he gently poured the rest of his koolade on the ground.

A VETERAN AT 24

LIFE ON A FIRE SUPPORT BASE

Fire Support Bases (FSB's) were dotted all over the Vietnam landscape. Their purpose was, just as the name implies, to serve as a base from which artillery could support infantry operations outside of the normal umbrella of coverage. They would go up in a matter of days, sometimes hours, and generally consisted of an artillery battery or two surrounded by sandbagged bunkers, concertina wire and infantry on the perimeter. They were the next step up from a Night Defensive Position (NDP) which was what we called the temporary location of an infantry unit when it stopped for the night and, most times, dug only shallow foxholes.

Life on a FSB could be very exciting when Charlie decided it was a target of opportunity or needed to be hit because the fire support was doing its job too well. Other times it was an incredibly dull and boring existence. I never did like them — too much of a stationary target! I preferred being on the move in the jungle where I had a degree of control over when and where we made contact!

August 19, 1968
FSB Judy
We're still at FSB Judy. My company had a 2 plt operation today but I stayed back! LT. Love the XO took it over.

Boy, my feet are bad. I have my boots off and a pair of captured VC sandals on. The flies are buzzing around my feet like it's rotten food or something.

I'm enclosing an overlay! I receive one similar to this just about every day as a company commander.

September 11–17, 1968

FSB & Location Unknown

I'm still improving the defenses of the FSB and being the CO of Echo Company.

Happiness is a paper cup full of ice cold vanilla ice cream at a very hot Fire Support Base in Vietnam. That's right! We got ice cream flown in today by chopper. They have an ice cream plant at Cu Chi and LTC Childs says that "we would have ice cream."

... we're on 100% alert now (it's 2330 hours) because the COL feels that we will get hit tonight. Enclosed is a picture of Ronnie Nelson and me sitting in the TOC in the afternoon. It was kind of a dull afternoon as you see by the expressions.

We've had a pretty exciting day today. We had 18 mortar rounds dropped in on us. We only had 5 lightly wounded. No sweat! At 2300 hours (it's midnight now) we were supposed to get hit by a ground and mortar attack, but no show. Maybe it's because we fired over 500 rounds of artillery fire around the FSB at 5 minutes to 11. I hope that he was out there all fat and happy waiting for 2300 when bam! It was pretty spectacular.

No sleep last night. Charlie tried to hit the FSB but never hurt us much. We took about 60 mortar rounds but I had only 4 lightly wounded (3 are back on duty). FSB Pope (3/187) to our north was hit by about 300 Charlies. Ronnie Nelson was there and got slightly wounded ... he took frags to the back just like someone else did once upon a time.

The Dance Will Begin Again

The gray dawn fades, giving way slowly.
Soon the heat will be back
carried on the bright light of an orange sun.
Seeping into every dark corner.

Blurred images from last night
gradually take shape and show color.
As if in a silent ballet synchronized with the sun's arrival,
black figures recede into the jungle.

The final act of their nightly dance is always the same.
Their exit tied to the sun by an unseen conductor's hand.
The faster the sun rises,
the quicker they disappear from view.
I have never seen them miss their cue,
nor linger on stage.

In the night, they are everywhere.
Sometimes inside the wire where we are.
By day they are gone,
nowhere to be seen.
Resting from last night's performance.
Rehearsing for another opening night.

In the dark,
you hear the symphony of sounds that accompanies
their dance.
The staccato of the machine guns serves as drums.
The crump of grenades provides bass.
Wind instruments are whistling booby traps,
before they explode.

Sometimes a solo voice performs.
The words make no sense
to the green soldiers inside the wire.
The words are singsong gibberish
to the frightened man-child from East LA
and the farmer's son from Iowa.
But the urgency and tone are unmistakable,
sometimes shouting in anger and or pain.

By day,
the symphony is silent and the soloist gone.
Replaced by jungle sounds of a National Geographic
Special, only with a sinister story line.

Tonight will be like the last.
As the sun goes down and darkness creeps in,
the curtain will go up
and the dance will begin again.

I carried a picture of my infant son, Ricky, in an oilskin, waterproof baggie in the left breast pocket of my jungle fatigues. Often, before starting the next mission, I would take it out for one last look.

A Soldier's Goodbye

Sleep, now sleep, until I come for you.
Breathe in soft whispers, one sigh, then two.

Little blue cap on a small peanut head.
All curled up in a corner of the bed.

Sweet baby lashes, infant Elvis lips.
A head full of magical pirate ships.

Wondering bright eyes and little monkey toes.
Dreams of pixie dust and a puppy's wet nose.

Quiet, now quiet, rest close to me.
Hide your face, let me be the one to see.

Close, now close, insanity is intense.
Father's goodbyes spoken on both sides of the fence.

Stay, now stay, safe again over my heart.
Far from this madness that's about to start.

Hospital Visit

You cheered me up.
It was supposed to be different.
I didn't step on the booby trap.
You did.

I had my arms.
Your right hand couldn't hold a coffee cup.
I was standing unsure of what to say.
You were in bed in pain;
joking about chasing nurses in a wheelchair.

I made promises to visit.
You smiled with wisdom beyond your 23 years.
Was it courage or morphine?
I wish I knew then, what I know now.

Stupid me.
It was courage.

VIEW FROM GROUND ZERO

Vietnam had a way of crystallizing one's thoughts. Complex social and political issues and subtle human emotions were reduced by an infantryman's logic to simple black and white basics. I had an opinion or stand on most every topic. Some appear very callous upon revisiting them thirty years later!

April 7, 1968

Rocket Belt (North of Bien Hoa)

... we heard about Martin Luther King and the riots in Washington, D.C. It's funny, but there is no racism or bigotry etc in a combat outfit, everyone fights the same, bleeds the same and dies the same. Can't these people in the USA see that?

April 12, 1968

Rocket Belt (North of Bien Hoa)

There's a big drive going on in Vietnam for the Vietnamese refugees from the TET Offensive. All the collections were voluntary. So far, my Company has given $10 and that was given by LT Matloz who hasn't been under fire yet. Here's my way of thinking. I haven't seen any big drive going on for the families of the men who died during this offensive (Like K of Tiger B), so why should I give money or ask my troops to give money to help the people we're fighting ... I know it sounds cold-hearted but I've seen dead paratroopers, while close to 3/4 of the Americans in Vietnam haven't been too involved in the dirty, bloody and cruel part of the war.

June 11, 1968

6th Convalescent Center (Cam Ranh Bay)

... let me tell you something that people say when someone they know gets killed over here.

When two people discuss someone else's death, I have been a party to this on far too many occasions, they are naturally grieved at the loss of their friend, but an undertone is there that, "he is gone now and there is nothing we can do or say that will bring him back." The question always arises, "How did he get it?" If the answer says — quick & no pain — then there is relief, in a queer sense almost joy. If the answer is slow, hard, etc there is deep gloom and sometimes voices waver and break. Too many times I have gone through this now familiar ritual with classmates or former instructors at West Point on recalling the deaths of my classmates. Most of them you never knew, but I knew them as individuals and human beings. I have lost many friends, more than I had imagined ...

Believe it or not some of my strongest moments away from you have come while in Church. I know that God is in Vietnam, so maybe he's in Hawaii too. Just drop into any church ... be it a weekday or a Sunday and see what I mean.

August 30, 1968

Unknown Location

You know a thought just struck me! Little do those peaceniks realize that a veteran of Vietnam such as myself wants peace much, much more than they ever could. Strange, isn't it? I can say from the bottom of my heart that I wish this war would come to an end. I defy any peace-nik, who has never served in a combat outfit in Vietnam, to make such a statement with the authentic deep feelings behind it. They just don't know ... When the rear detachment received the KIA list I had a 19-year-old kid (who has been through it all) come up to me with tears in his eyes and say in a broken whisper "Sir, do you think this damned war will ever end?" That "kid" has every right in the world to go home and become a peace-nik because he knows & he feels! But not those bums that have never served. Sometimes there is no justice in this cruel world.

November 18, 1968

Vicinity Highway 1 (I Corps)

My personal opinion on the bombing halt is that it is a mistake. We are only giving our enemy a chance to recover, regroup and PRE-PARE. The only thing that people at my level think, and it is natural we're the ones that suffer the consequences of any concessions, is that we're waiting for the time (my estimate is 2–3 months from the bombing halt) when Charlie comes roaring out of his sanctuaries and the country erupts. We will stop him and defeat him I know, but the cost will be too high because of the bombing halt. I'm old-fashioned. I feel that we should go to the peace table with a string of victories and a history of unrelenting pressure on the enemy as our credentials, NOT making concessions and letting the enemy act as if their presence is a favor to us. The fierce pride that the soldier feels over here apparently has not reached the top level of our government. Our armies on the field of battle are hard, strong and ruthless. It is unfortunate that our policy makers are not the same. So go my thoughts for the night.

FNG

The newcomer's face brightens as he sees the short-timer
standing in line at the Base Camp Exchange. He walks up
to him and speaks:

"What unit are you with?"   *"101st."*

"Damn — you guys have seen a lot of shit."
"Heard you just came out of War Zone D."
"Bet that was something."
"How long have you been on the line?"   *"A year."*

"You must have been there for Tet!"
"Wish I had seen that — fighting everywhere;
  VC all around."
"Bet it was a blast — lots of stories to tell, huh?"
"Something to tell your grandkids."   *Silence.*

"Hey man — got any VC flags?
"I promised my girl one."
"I'll get one in a few days, no sweat."
"But, you got any to sell?"

Never looking up, the short-timer keeps picking at the
bamboo scabs on his arms and mutters,
                   "Fucking new guy." (FNG)

Dorothy Parker Didn't Write This

Three things I treasure to this day:
West Point classmates,
sergeant's advice and
ranger training in the red Georgia clay.

Three memories I would as soon give back:
poncho wrapped bodies,
killing zones and
crouching helpless under a night mortar attack.

LAST LETTER

You would expect my last letter from Vietnam to be a dramatic accounting of a full year in combat. Actually, it was a short, anticlimactic note written on pages ripped from a small, pocket notebook. This last letter happened to be written on my son's first birthday. In his first year of life I had been with him for only 20 days. I was more than ready to go home.

November 26, 1968

Camp Evans Base Camp (I Corps)

I'm finally writing my last letter in Vietnam. I never thought that this day would come. Just think in a few days ... only a few days.

Happy birthday to the finest son in the world from his very proud father!

What Was It Like In Vietnam?

Men of character acting like babies,
contrasted with
low life characters standing up like men.

Endless nights, boring patrols and dead days
punctuated by
chance contacts, savage firefights and brutally quick
ambushes.

Young men taking the lead, and old men thankful
it's not them,
replaced by
old men becoming the glue when the young fall apart.

Vivid, life-altering memories, made in an instant,
turned into just another war story
when the next awful moment comes, and the next
and the next.

Safety and comfort of bunkers, barbed wire and base camps
transformed into magnets
for mortar shells, sappers and snipers.

The dull sameness of a hundred jungle trails
electrified instantly
by finding a fresh boot print — not made in the USA.

Weeks of training and the mantra of relax/exhale/squeeze
forgotten in a heartbeat
the first time you shoot at another human being.

Upbringing, religion and all thoughts of the worth
of a human life
forgotten in a heartbeat
the first time you shoot at another human being.

Compassion for anyone not wearing US Army
jungle fatigues
lost in a moment
the first time you lift a poncho wrapped body of a buddy
into a chopper.

The ability to cry and feel and grieve
regained over a lifetime.
Slowly, imperceptibly — perhaps never completely.

Orient Express

Saddle up! Get ready for a monster ride.
You, and several hundred thousand of your closest friends,
are off on an all-expense paid trip on the Orient Express.
Get your tickets stamped, punched, spindled and mutilated.
Linger too long at one stop and miss the next train out,
maybe even the last train.

First stop on your personalized itinerary is Phuoc Vinh,
where ramshackle is raised to a fine art.
Check your orders and check your weapons.
Think Dodge City, only hotter.

Further down the line are Trang Bang, Trung Lap and Cu Chi.
Watch your step.
Watch your buddy.
Watch that tree line.
Hell, watch everything!

Be sure not to miss your all-inclusive side trips.

The scenic Mekong Delta,
where you notice our tracks run completely under water.
That's the wet, smelly brown liquid seeping into your boots.

The always exciting Rocket Belt,
where the local residents put on a nightly fireworks display,
just for you and the fly boys across the Dong Nai River.

Of course, who will ever forget
the legendary War Zone D for not one,
not two, but three glorious, fun-filled adventures.

Also, don't miss the spectacular sights and sounds
of festive Tet in downtown Bien Hoa.
Mind the burning buildings, now.

Stay awake. No sleeping on this ride, the best is yet to come.

As an unexpected bonus, here comes another spontaneous
side trip.
How could one traveler be so lucky?
You and your companions are being whisked away to an
undisclosed destination in
— "Yes, that's a drum roll!" — the Central Highlands.
There, you will have a secret rendezvous with your
Uncle Charles
and all his cousins, friends, acquaintances, school chums
and anyone else, it seems, he may have run in to along the way.

Your first mountain resort stop is Dak To, then off to Dak Pek,
known for steep mountains, thick jungles and chilly nights.
Let's not forget the magical, mystical visits from Puff the
Magic Dragon
and the always popular, death defying Arc Light displays.

Finally, a life-altering, brief layover at Fire Support Base 25,
that little blip on the map well past remote,
for a surprise reunion with your West Point leadership
instructor "Ranger".
Be especially mindful of your welcoming committee's
mortars, rifles,
machine guns and recoilless rifles.
Ooops! Did I fail to mention hand grenades?
Sorry. Looks like one of those bad mothers sent you to the
docs at Pleiku

to have your shirt cut off, or what was left of it.
Damn, you stink! Those shell holes full of muddy water not
a good enough bath tub for you?
Then on to Cam Ranh Bay for three wonderful weeks in
bed, wearing funky blue pajama bottoms.

Now, if you don't mind, back to our planned itinerary.

You have rejoined the tour just in time for a trip to, yes,
you guessed it
another "drum roll" — the A Shau Valley.
What an honor to finally make it to the gateway to
South Vietnam
Don't thank me. You deserve this and more and we aim to
give it to you.
So, bend over and hang on!

Whether it is waiting out mortar attacks at night
or guarding Highway 525 during the day,
we have first-class accommodations waiting for you
at a string of luxurious fire support bases —
Bastogne, Birmingham and Vehgel.
Hope you don't mind your four-legged roommates.
Rats need a place to sleep, as well.

Your last stop is base camp at Hue/Phu Bai.
That's your spot in the ditch over there.
Follow the crowd when the nightly fireworks start,
and they will!

Well, you made it.
Your tour with us is over.
Hell of a ride, wasn't it?
Can't wait to see the pictures.
Bye Bye.
Y'all come back, now.

AFTERMATH AND AFTERSHOCKS

Silent Too Long

I write
because I have been silent too long.
The walls I have so carefully built
can no longer hold the emotions I so fervently feel.

I write
because I am alive when the pen moves.

I write
because I can revisit old friends and deep wounds
on the same long plane ride across the Pacific.
Sometimes hurling myself headfirst into the minefields
of my memories
or testing first with my toe, then pulling back.

I write
because I can be silly and light.
With no purpose but to capture my little girl's journey
through life,
where even the discovery of a ladybug is a
priceless moment.

I write
because I can.
Somehow knowing that the time spent in reflection
on each word and message moves me that much closer
to who I want to be.

I write
because you will read it,
understand me,
accept me,
and love me,
not for what I went through
but how I came through it.

Your War is Over

Put your rifle up on the wall my friend.
Your war is over.
You talk as if the blood still flows red
and the jungle rot festers in raw patches.

Those wounds have long ago healed,
even the scars have faded.
The welcome parade is expected any day now,
with bands playing and flags snapping
and people actually proud to see you back.
It will never come.

The ache you feel for missing friends is fresh and real.
They came home long ago to rest
in a quiet place of stones and straight lines.

War movies stir your memories.
You stay away.
Vietnam books are too painful.
You don't turn the pages.
They are just someone else's images, not yours.

Your loved ones feel the sting of your words
and confusion over the distance you keep.
Your reasons are lost in your past.
They carry more years than the ages of your children.
Yes, my friend, put your rifle up on the wall.

Your war is over.

Somewhat Haiku

It is not all dark,
the outlook I gained from
my Vietnam tour.

Coming close to death
means holding tighter to life.
Some things just mean more.

The first shot attempt
by a skinny freshman guard
right before the half.

A nightly tale of
yellow monkeys and Toby
told to help her sleep.

Hot tea, sipped slow
on a cold December day,
watching the first snow.

Old time rock and roll
at Muldoon's with cold beer
on a summer night.

Tall trees, pale blue sky,
warm breezes and holding hands,
with no words passed.

A quiet sunrise
standing in a dewy field,
with a little dog.

Shared life's secrets
over a bottle of red,
feeling who you are.

A child's sleepy call
from her ladybug quilt,
"Mama and Daddy."

Running in the cold.
Muscles warm, rhythm just right.
Jumping ice patches.

The call from a son
after a long nine month's wait,
"You are a Pa Pa."

Cross country skiing.
Trying to outrun the sounds
of my skis sliding.

Pride of a small boy
back from a Hartz mountain trek
 with a pack his size.

Seeing my father
in two son's values and yes,
even in my own.

Waiting for the dip
of a brilliant sunset.
Loving the North Shore.

Tutu's beach birthdays,
wrinkled aunts, happy hour and
love everywhere.

A stranger's handshake
on Memorial Day with
a quiet, "Thank you."

Shuffling Off to Nowhere

Fearless.
How everyone saw you.
It wasn't the swagger.
Everyone with time in the bush swaggered.
It was the look.
The confidence.
The control when everything turned to crap.
The VC couldn't touch you.
Lifers never tamed you.
You were born for combat.
A Viking marauder carrying an M16.

Boundless.
What your horizons were.
Your tour was just one year
Give it everything — go all out.
Then back to the states and party,
school, a job.
It was all in the plan.
Vietnam was a short detour on what was sure to be
a full and exciting life.
You couldn't miss.

Emotionless.
How you felt.
Ten lifetimes of crippling memories seared into a young brain.
Eighty-eight days of back to back missions.
Three straight weeks of contact.
Thirty plus combat assaults.
No time to ask, why?
Why me?

You couldn't grieve for a friend
or even shudder at what you saw
when choppers were in-bound for yet another
combat assault.
You just shut down.
As one of your counselors explained it,
you were stopped in your tracks emotionally
and never able to start up again.

Heartless.
What your ex-wife called you at the custody hearing.
A broken marriage and two children
heading down their own self-destructive paths,
left behind with only some regret.
Lucky for them the judge had them live with their mother.
It was easier to hide the drugs and booze in the
earlier years
when you only had to be sober every other weekend.
Later it wouldn't matter.
You couldn't hide it anymore
and you didn't try.

Aimless.
How the VA center labeled you.
Two false starts in college
and a string of dead end jobs.
Each one lower on the scale than the last.
Ten lost days in a Dallas jail
after a fight at a strip club.
Nothing seemed to work.
Not your fault,
just a string of bad luck,
you explained to anyone who would listen.

Clueless.
What you called everyone who wasn't a vet.
They all tried to help.
But, you never opened up.
Never tried.
Never cried.
It was at the VA when you first heard what it was.
Post Traumatic Stress Disorder.
Big deal, it has a name!
So what.
You still couldn't hold a job,
or the love of a good woman
or the respect of your children.

Homeless.
How you ended up.
Living day to day.
Always seeking a better place to sleep.
Mostly it's the 12th Street shelter on cold nights.
Sometimes the north side bridge is the place.
It has a few dry sleeping spots.
The cops don't patrol it much.
Food is once a day.
Twice if you are lucky.
The missions and churches help.
Sometimes you forget to go,
or were too high, or both.
Mostly you just spend your days
shuffling off to nowhere,
leaving unnoticed,
arriving unwanted.

Senseless.
What the papers called your death.
You were found curled up in a doorway
only three blocks from a shelter with empty beds.
You were alone on a sub-zero night.
You would have been a John Doe
but for the faded newspaper clipping,
carefully folded and wrapped in plastic,
with a picture of two small children
clutching teddy bears at Christmas past.
The article sparkled about your glory days
as a 19 year-old, full of life.
And your Bronze Star.
And Purple Heart.
Back, when you were
Fearless.

Memorial Day

We are free because
others paid the full price.
Freedom is partly mine;
I own a small piece.

Men under my command
were hit and some did die.
I am at peace
because in Vietnam, I did try.

Our young men and women
who went off to war were this nation's best.
I am proud to have stood with them
and passed the same test.

The color guard today
reminds me of ceremonies gone by,
when I didn't feel
or want to cry.

Now I feel
and sometimes cry, too.
So, thank this quiet soldier
when I speak to you.

Silent Movies

Tell me how the wounds bleed bright red blood,
flowing out,
spreading into pools,
staining clothes and grass,
stopping only on its own terms.

Tell me of the cries of wounded soldiers
from pain when bullets hit
or fear when death comes close.
Sometimes words — often only sounds.

Tell me of all these sights and sounds
that should be in my memory
in blazing color and ringing clarity.
Vivid and real.

Now tell me sir,
why my dreams are silent movies?
Stark black and white images,
silently moving across the screen.

Homecoming

Looking up over tea,
and a crossword puzzle,
she sees his face.
From her chair on the sun porch,
wearing the summer beach house like a faded, favorite hat,
she smiles.

She sees what they all do,
leaner now and bronzed,
and oh, so handsome.
Eyes of the morning sky.
Lips shaped around soft words.
Fewer now, still soft, though.
A youthful swagger to his walk,
befitting a young warrior's return.

She feels in him what they cannot.
Winter storms boiling and cold, dark clouds forming.
Signaling intermittent squalls rolling in off an angry sea.
One line slamming the coast
as another forms, just out of sight.
Strangely absent are the shrieking winds.

His quietness mistaken for tranquility.

Sensing danger she rises
to confront the unknown.
A long dormant Irish temper flares,
fueled by a she bear's instincts.
Her rage matches the storm's fury.
"Where is my gentle son?
What have you done with him?
Speak to me! I want an answer!"
In the silence, she has her answer.
Reluctantly, she settles back.

Her acceptance mistaken for tranquility.

Do You Ever Miss It?

Do you ever miss it?
The feeling of being truly alive after coming close to death.
When your senses are at the outer limits.
When all you can do is exhale,
wondering what in the hell just happened.

Do you ever look for it in other places?
That adrenaline rush when you heard the cry of "incoming"
or "we are in contact."
That quick jolt of fear that followed the crack of a round
over your head
and you knew it was close.

Do you ever try to recreate it?
That pure, simple bond between soldiers in combat that is
stronger than death.
When you trusted that your buddy would be there, even if
he was in the line of fire.
When you knew, without looking, that he had your back.

Before you give me the quick answer,
the one you've used all these years.
Look deep into the corners of your soul.
Go deeper!
Past the layers accumulated from fifty years of civilization.
Go back to who you were, back then.

Now, answer me.
Just as I thought,
me too.

Small Prescence

Once lost, now found.
Feelings set aside, picked up again.
Dusted off, looked at with curiosity.
Tried out to see if a fit is there.
Seeing the response, knowing it is right.
Tried again, maybe a habit one day.

Would it be different, if I hadn't gone?
Would passion play a part, if I had stayed home?
Was it combat?
Has it been me all along?

Questions too deep for answers.
Answers too frightening to hear.
Feelings too fragile to be tested.
Life's path too winding to be understood.

The search goes on.
Still more feelings to uncover.
More passions to enflame.
A small, fresh presence to help.
She opens doors in houses I didn't know existed,
on streets I never dreamed were there.

She takes my hand.
We walk through the door together.

ABOUT THE AUTHOR

Rick St John is a 1966 graduate of West Point who served in Vietnam with the 101st Airborne Division during some of the war's heaviest fighting. He is also author of *Tiger Bravo's War: An epic year with an elite airborne rifle company of the 101st Airborne Division's "Wandering Warriors,"* during the height of the Vietnam war. With two successful careers behind him, retiring as a US Army Colonel in 1993 and as a Group Executive of a global financial transactions processing company in 2012, Rick spends his time teaching and writing.

Left: Rick St John, outside Tiger Bravo headquarters, Phuoc Vinh Base Camp, date unknown. Right: Rick St. John today.